Why Binding Python Doesn't Work

The Spirit of Python 101

By
Paula Cross

© Copyright 2017 - Paula Cross

All right reserved. This book is protected by the copyright laws of the United States of America. This book may not be copied or reprinted. Please inquire for volume discount pricing.

Ebooks – Licensing for ebook distribution to entire congregations or bible study groups are available. $30 per Bible Study Group or House Church. $50 per Congregation under 75 members. $100 per Congregation of 76-250 members. $150 per Congregation of 251-1000 members. $200 per Congregation 1001+ members. Please inquire at lasthourpublications@gmail.com.

Cover: Photos by Tiberiu Sahlean, a contributing photographer of Dreamstime.com. Cover Layout Design by Paula Cross. Disclaimer: The usage of images is not necessarily an endorsement of the photographers other artistic endeavors.

Last Hour Publications
Monroeville, PA 15146
lasthourpublications@gmail.com

TABLE OF CONTENTS

Chapter 1:
The Spirit of Python 101 – Page 5

Chapter 2:
Binding & Loosing – Page 15

Chapter 3:
Then & Now: The Truth About Spiritual Warfare – Page 23

Chapter 4:
When Casting Out Python Does and *Doesn't* Work – Page 39

Summary:
Final Words – Page 49

-Chapter 1-

THE SPIRIT OF PYTHON 101

When people discover that the spirit of python is the one behind the distress in their lives, they want simple A, B, C instructions on getting rid of him. The best we've come up with is binding python, casting him out or cutting off his head. But when it comes to binding and casting out spirits, we've gotten way off kilter and found... *it doesn't work.*

Technically, it should be easy to overcome python but we've been suckers for his strategies, and (unwittingly) deeply intertwined with dark kingdom policies.

Further, we think of the spirit of python as one single entity that is implementing the particular assault that's constricting us – be it lethargy or relentless financial complications or otherwise. There are countless ways constriction can manifest in people's lives. But that's not where the complexity comes into play. The complexity is that the spirit of python, being the breath taker, is *the counterfeit of the Holy Spirit*, and he administers demonic spirits to accomplish his mission. For example, say you have a spirit of self-hatred. God will reveal it as a snake, namely python, because the self-hatred-spirit's end goal isn't that you hate yourself only, but so that the counterfeit of the Holy Spirit has access to constrict, oppress, and suffocate you more. The snake God showed you is how He is revealing to you that python has acquired access to you which, in this example, was accomplished via the spirit of self-hatred. If you see numerous snakes, God is showing you there are multiple spirits that are working together to give the counterfeit of the Holy Spirit, python, extensive access.

Think about it... The more you yield to bad attitudes, pride, selfishness, spitefulness, whatever, the less comfort, peace and guidance you have from the Holy Spirit, the less you're able to worship and pray, and the more discomfort and oppression you have from Holy Spirit's counterfeit.

The added complexity in dealing with the spirit of python is most people have many different spirits they're vulnerable to and struggling with. Therefore, the constricting counterfeit's access is profound. You should appreciate that this is why it cannot be an A, B, C deliverance in most cases. Attending deliverance meetings isn't likely to unveil all the areas through which you've been giving python access to your life. It's possible but not the norm because there's a lifetime of wrong, false programming needing addressed; much of which is rooted deep in your soul. Remember, salvation is something we work out via being transformed by the renewing of our minds. This includes recognizing deep-seated false programming. The deeper we get saturated in God's Word, then, owning and possessing it, the quicker the transformation and deliverance process. If python's authority is due to a single, huge door such as unforgiveness, for example, and he has no other gateways of false prominence in your soul, this would be all it takes to cut him off. Unfortunately, there are typically many doors. And though God would gladly reveal all the doors in a single session, it's too much to face all at once for most. Not to mention we just might not be willing to admit certain things to ourselves yet. The bottom line is our determination for and application of the truths we learn are what qualifies and prepares us to face more. Let me emphasize that it's the *resolve for* and *application of truths* that cuts python off. I know this for a fact. I'm living proof.

Further, deliverance sessions and being prayed over may not serve to teach you how to come out of agreement with the spirits you've been one with all your life. Ministers can cast demons out of you all day but deep down if you still agree with the lies, they come back! Your confidence in their suggestions is their open door. Not fully believing what God says in the matter and applying the truth of it is laying out the red carpet to dark authority. This is why overcoming the spirit of python is complex. It's not about a simple trespassing spirit that needs cast out only. It's about your affiliation with various spirits that is granting the dark kingdom jurisdiction over you. It's a situation that YOU need to come out of, not the reverse. This is a process that requires diligence. You may not like this, but despite sincerely making Jesus your Lord and Savior, the more infatuated with or disillusioned by dark kingdom policies you are (including things like self-pity, worry, doubting God's love, self-hatred, negative self-talk, insecurity, pride, loving this life and its comforts, etc.), the more your experiential victory over python is stifled. Everything is contingent upon which kingdom you operate in. The battle between our flesh and spirit is intense, in deed, but the power of Christ is our weapon and our arsenals are loaded. Yet we subconsciously prefer dark policies and assume having the Name of Jesus in our back pockets should be enough. It simply doesn't work like this. (This may be difficult for some to hear. Ask the Lord to help you fully embrace the truth of this before you read on.)

Meanwhile, just how do we know for sure that python is, in fact, the counterfeit of the Holy Spirit? Well, we know that Satan counterfeits everything God does. Therefore, since God is Father, Son and Holy Spirit, Satan is also a father (John 8:44), and uses the spirit of antichrist and the false prophet as his son and spiritual activist to do his bidding similar to how Father God sent Jesus and Holy Spirit to do His. I refer to the spirit of antichrist and the false prophet as Satan's Generals. They aren't three in one, but they do their best to mimic it. At any rate, think about what the Holy Spirit does for believers and then compare it to what His counterfeit does...

The Bible says Holy Spirit is our comforter, teacher, guide, and He ALWAYS points us to Jesus Christ. You know how John 4:24 says, *"God is a Spirit: and they that worship him must worship him **in** spirit and in truth"*? This means when we're truly worshiping, it's in unity with and of the Holy Spirit! Meaning, Holy Spirit's breath *is* our worship! Additionally, Holy Spirit gives believers supernatural gifts at His discretion. He performs miracles and is the power source flowing through a believer when somebody is supernaturally healed, raised from the dead, delivered, etc. When a believer speaks in unknown tongues, Holy Spirit is the One giving the believer "utterance".

On the contrary, the false prophet (the big guy spoken of in Revelation 16:13) is the one that ALWAYS points people to the antichrist and everything false. He's the one that steals our worship! The false prophet (the

"3rd person" of the demonic trinity) is the one that steals our peace, guides us into lies and problems, teaches us false doctrines and the worship of false gods, and even self), performs false miracles (they're real, but serve a false, agenda), and gives people FALSE utterance (supernatural tongues that contradict God's truth one way or another), and false interpretation. The false prophet's role, alongside the spirit of antichrist and their father, Satan, is to counter Holy Spirit. And his job is to not only counter all that Holy Spirit does, but to constrict the entire body of Christ, squeezing the breath of God out of them. This is how he got his nickname, Python.

Python's job is to squeeze the life of God and HIS SPIRIT or BREATH or POWER out of true believers. Evidence that the spirit of python is one and the same as Revelation 16:13's false prophet is Acts 16:16. The woman was operating in the supernatural power of "false utterance". Who but the false prophet oversees the workings of divination and false prophecy? The Apostle Paul called the author of the damsel's false utterance, "Python". Why would Paul address a divination spirit as a snake – except that God was revealing his true identity.

But the spirit of python doesn't only operate via false utterance. He operates by implementing, promoting and pointing to anything false, as stated previously. Python (the false prophet / counterfeit of Holy Spirit) will, therefore, appoint demons of all sorts to lure people into false beliefs (such as, 'God doesn't care', etc.), teach them false doctrine, suck them into false practices (spirit of religion!), perform false miracles, wrap them up in idolatry and false worship - anything false. As unsuspecting saints yield to these, the Spirit or breath, even the river of God in them, becomes constricted. They may feel it, even the sense of suffocating. They may experience the walls of their lives closing in on them. Or they may feel great, thinking everything is hunky dory, having no clue the supernatural power they operate in is of the devil. They see all these miracles, but do they help others become more like Jesus as a result, having clear, fruit evidence of God's Kingdom which is righteousness, peace and joy...patience, humility, long suffering and self-control? These are the real indicators of the Holy Spirit in a believer. If Holy Spirit is thriving, His fruits aren't constricted.

At any rate, one saint's constriction will manifest one way while another saint's constriction will manifest another. At the end of the day, it doesn't matter. Python's job is to make sure the demons figure out what works best against YOU. Just so long as you're heading down a false path deeper into their clutches where python can squeeze tighter and tighter until you get to the point where you think you're dying and can't go on, or to where you're just plain useless for God's Kingdom. Python has the same end goal for all believers, regardless of the path he must take to get each of us there.

The first book I wrote, The Spirit of Python Unveiled, explains all of the above in greater depth. It teaches about python's actual identity, his many faces, his origins, who he's after, and the signs or symptoms that indicate he has a hold. It also lays out his strategies, how he's able to dominate Christians in the first place, general keys to coming out of his grip, and my personal one-on-one journey with Holy Spirit out of python's dominion. It's very informative. But I've come to realize most people are so severely dominated by python that they can't focus enough to read such a complicating book. I admit, it can be very overwhelming for many. Especially for those who are at their end. I realize they need the short of it. So that's what this book is about.

I've spoken to many constricted believers these past few years since the release of The Spirit of Python Unveiled. Many share how they've worked with deliverance ministers and have been prayed over numerous times to no avail. They say either nothing helps at all or that things improve momentarily only to go back to how things were before, or worse.

The problem is we haven't understood the simplicity of victory over darkness. The corporate body of Christ is teaching and exercising half-truths that only serve to increase bondage. Evil spirits are able to use these inadequacies to gain more and more ground. Deliverance sessions are often times a playground for darkness. The spirit of python has the run of the mill in many a case and he loves how his victims repeatedly throw themselves out in front of the bus. Doing the same things over and over, getting nowhere, and coming back for more.

We've turned 'deliverance' into a smorgasbord of exercises and given the kingdom of darkness a greater platform through which to work. Meanwhile, the truth is very simple to understand. The Lord reveals through His Word how to come out of python's play land and into His stability. It's time we do. We need to get this, already.

It's for these reasons I'm going to cut straight to the chase and explain why binding and casting out python, or any evil spirit for that matter, won't work. And you're going to understand the truth of why, instead of trampling over every work of the enemy, we're the ones who are being trampled!

I hope your approach to this short read includes determination to receive and apply its truths. God has been patient with us. The irony is many of us have blamed the Lord for our distress, wondering why He won't help us. Meanwhile, He's displeased that we're suffering at the hand of the very darkness He defeated. He handed us keys on a silver platter and we're taking fits on Him because we're not minding what's on the platter. We have tried His patience long enough. We have put His sacrifice to shame long enough. Let's stop playing around. Let's take responsibility for our actions and be resolved in the truth.

-Chapter 2-

Binding & Loosing

Despite all the hype concerning binding and loosing, there are only three situations in scripture where they are reflected upon, and none of them substantiate the running trend. We're going to look closely at these passages, beginning with Matthew 18:15-19.

> *"If your brother or sister sins against you, go and point out their fault, just between the two of you. If they listen to you, you have won them over. But if they will not listen, take one or two others along, so that 'every matter may be established by the testimony of two or three witnesses.' If they still refuse to listen, tell it to the church; and if they refuse to listen even to the church, consider them as you would a pagan or a tax collector.*
>
> *"Truly I tell you, whatever you bind on earth will be bound in*

heaven, and whatever you loose on earth will be loosed in heaven.

"Again, truly I tell you that if two of you on earth agree about anything they ask for, it will be done for them by my Father in heaven. For where two or three gather in my name, there am I with them."

This passage reminds me of John 20:23 where Jesus appeared to the disciples and told them that if they forgive anyone of their sins, they're forgiven; if they do not, they aren't.

Back then the Pharisees were the ones that had all the say and the Messiah constantly challenged this. But now it was no longer just about the insanity of Jesus forgiving people of their sins that the Pharisees had to contend with – but the audacity of *commoners* having such authority that surpassed their own, as well! Both these passages are about Jesus granting very serious, divine power to the disciples. This was a direct assault against the Pharisees. *"Whatever you little people who believe in Me bind or loose, done. Whatever two or more of you small timers agree upon, done. Whoever you forgive, done. Whoever you don't, not done."* –Whoa.

But what exactly did Jesus mean by binding and loosing? We have to look at the context of the passage which begins with Jesus instructing them on how to deal with a believer who won't receive correction. After telling them to count the offender as a pagan if they refuse correction, that's when Jesus says whatever they bind or loose is a done deal in the heavens. And then Jesus elaborates further saying if they agree concerning something, it's done as well.

We, therefore, cannot isolate the binding and loosing verse as its own thing. It absolutely cannot stand alone. Since it had something to do with the believer that wouldn't receive correction who is now counted as an unbeliever, we have to figure out how it correlates.

Our understanding of binding and loosing refers to restraining or releasing something, but this doesn't fit the context of the passage. After all, how do we restrain or release a believer that's gone bad? I was left hanging over this for years until I discovered what a woman named Lonnie Lane explained re: binding and loosing, and then it all made sense.

As you may already know, Lonnie Lane reveals how the Greek terms in this passage that mean 'bind' and 'loose' actually mean 'forbid' and 'permit' in Hebrew. She explains how the High Priests had been the only ones allowed to exercise authority over what is and isn't permitted in the Torah, but that now Jesus was overriding this. I imagine people were so accustomed to the High Priests determining if someone was in sin that believers in Christ would never presume the right to assess or 'judge' a fellow believer as we ought (1 Corinthians 5:12). Yet here was the Messiah telling them that from then on, they absolutely were at liberty to do so.

In Matthew 16:18 where Jesus told Peter He was giving him the keys to the Kingdom of Heaven, and that whatever he bound or loosed on earth would be likewise in the heavens, what Jesus was actually saying is that whatever Peter (being a believer who had the revelation of the Messiah) forbids or permits is what will be forbidden or permitted in the heavens. Again, the disciples and all of Judea knew the High Priests were the only ones strictly qualified with such authority. But Jesus was saying the authority of the High Priests (being unbelievers without the revelation of the Messiah) had no spiritual backing unlike His Church now had!

Now that I understood that Jesus was actually saying "forbid and permit", Matthew 18:18 finally made sense. Jesus was telling them, *"If a brother or sister sins against you, take it to them privately. If that doesn't work, take two witnesses. If that doesn't work, tell the church. If they still refuse correction, count them as a pagan. You (the Church) are at liberty to forbid them from counting as one with you, and the heavens will count it as such as well. In fact, whatever you (the Church) agree about concerning the brother or sister in question is backed by Heaven also. You're requests will be granted concerning the matter."*

Wow. Now that makes sense!

With all that said, if Lonnie Lane is correct, binding and loosing is actually forbidding and permitting which explains why Jesus never personally executed 'binding' or 'loosing' against Satan or any demons...ever. He cast out many demons, yes. He rebuked Satan (Matthew 16:23). And He refuted and resisted Satan's temptations in the desert by declaring, *"It is written..."* But Jesus never bound an enemy of darkness. Jesus never commanded any demons to "loose" people, either. In fact, the only time he referred to someone being loosed was the woman in Luke 13:12. And that was no different than saying, *"Woman, you are released."* It had nothing to do with commanding the infirmity to loose her.

Since we cannot substantiate the doctrine of binding and loosing we've been following, we must throw it out. There's no spiritual backing for it. None. Indeed, Jesus did say in Matthew 12:29 and Mark 3:27 that nobody can enter a strongman's house and plunder it unless he first *binds* the strongman. But this was in correlation with the Pharisees accusing Jesus of casting out demons by the power of Beelzebul. Jesus was pointing out that the last thing Satan would do is grant Jesus permission to invade his house. That's why

Jesus said He'd have to bind Satan first to accomplish such a feat. If Satan was cool with Jesus knocking around his demons, that would mean he was willfully surrendering his kingdom – which obviously wasn't the case. Therefore, these passages don't show Jesus instructing us to bind Satan. They show Jesus explaining why He couldn't possibly cast demons out by the power of the devil.

The bottom line is there is no binding and loosing of any sort directed towards the enemy in the Bible. It always had to do with people dealing with people. When Jesus or the apostles took authority over dark powers, it was an instruction to come out, go, leave, and the like. It's for this reason that we cannot continue on with this "binding demons/Satan" doctrine. The doctrine of Christ was casting out demons, not binding them. That's not to say the Holy Spirit might not have you forbid (bind) a demon to continue in its pursuit but surely, this would be in conjunction with getting rid of it (casting it out). But that's not what we've been doing. We've been running around like madmen with ropes and handcuffs, binding all these powers, yet allowing them to remain on the premises! Or we waste time binding when all we have to do, through the power of the Spirit, is say, "GO!"

Again, I'm not saying Holy Spirit won't ever forbid a spirit but this absolutely isn't protocol. It certainly was the approach laid out in scripture. If Jesus never did it, how can we presume that we can create a doctrine out of it, making it our primary recourse against powers of darkness?

That which we (who have the revelation of the Messiah) forbid or permit on earth concerning matters of the Church is likewise forbidden or permitted in the heavens (spirit realm).

There's no such thing as chaining or handcuffing the devil and his minions in the Bible so this was never meant to be our system of approach like it's become. When we consider the only binding God ever executed was against angels that abandoned their origins, leaving their appointed habitation (Jude 1:6, 2 Peter 2:4) and had to do with chaining to the abyss. And the only binding yet to be done is the angel that comes down to bind Satan in chains to the bottomless pit for a thousand years (Revelation 20:2). These dark entities are bound to specific locations for specific time periods. When we bind spirits, I know it's for the sake of restricting them and not confining them to an cell or some other place. But again, it wasn't the practice of Jesus Christ and His first appointees who walked in His authority.

Of course, we are told to take our thoughts captive (2 Corinthians 10:5). Our thoughts may be inspired by demons but note that what we are told to take captive is the thought, not the demon(s) that perpetuated it!

Does this not speak volumes? Does this not illustrate how well we've mangled up how we are supposed to contend with evil?

Again, it's not to say we won't forbid a demon something at some time or another. I don't want to make it sound like it's heretical to do so. I can't say this would be 'wrong'. What's wrong is turning binding demons into a doctrine and routine protocol when it has no Biblical basis.

So it stands to reason... We need to scrap the whole binding and loosing doctrine. It's not substantiated in the Word of God and needs to be thrown out. Forbid strictly when Holy Spirit says so, but ditch the doctrine.

-Chapter 3-

THE TRUTH ABOUT SPIRITUAL WARFARE

Considering how off kilter we've been regarding Kingdom of God authority as well as binding and loosing, it would do us well to take a broader look at the corporate body's overall system and see how it compares to the original Church, and enhance our understanding as to just how far we've wandered. This will help us make sense of why so many of us believers have been so easily manipulated by darkness and have been under his feet instead of him being under ours, through Christ.

Let's face it... The Church systems of today don't look like the program Jesus ran back in His day. Especially since there were no programs. Things were simple: Preach the good news, demonstrate the power of the Kingdom when opportunities arise, make disciples of new believers, and cast out demons when necessary. As far as miracles and deliverance were concerned, these were a part of introducing or demonstrating the Kingdom of God. They were never anything to be prostituted; they were never meant to be the focus. Jesus and the Apostles would miraculously meet needs to demonstrate the reality of the Kingdom in conjunction with guiding people to salvation. Then they'd move on.

As Jesus traveled and met people where they were, the miracles, likewise, followed Him in order to demonstrate the Kingdom of God. Later Paul and the other Apostles followed His example. Miracles were never meant to be localized movements. The only localized movement was the daily gathering of believers for the sake of quality fellowship, Communion, discipleship, holding one another accountable, bearing one another's burdens, worshiping God in unity, mentoring the young, serving one another, and praying for each other. The simplicity of these criteria seems to have been lost. Weekly church services and conference gatherings touch on them, yes. But other 'stuff' has been placed ahead of them. Meanwhile, the purpose for localized gatherings was so that believers would become mature, attaining to the whole, full stature of Christ (Ephesians 4:13). There were no miracle or deliverance conferences. That's not to say it's wrong to have them. The point is it's not how Jesus or the early Church did things, so we have to consider how little these contribute to bringing believers into Christ's full stature. Judging by the lack of authority across the board, how much the Church looks like the world, and the measure of defeat throughout the Church, it's safe to say today's system and practices aren't cutting it.

Again, there's very little about today's church system that does bring believers into the full stature of Christ. The average church sees few, if any, miracles or deliverances. And almost nobody understands spiritual warfare. Instead, many believers are confused or in bondage. Most believers remain vulnerable to sickness and disease, and very few are mature enough to administer the power of God to a hurting and hopeless generation. Worse, many believers themselves are oppressed and tormented by darkness. This is not how the Church is supposed to be.

With that said, how can we expect the Church to be victorious concerning spiritual warfare? Believers either avoid the topic altogether or get caught up in battling the devil by rebuking him, binding him, and commanding him. This is how I've heard believers dealing with the enemy for decades but the truth is the Bible doesn't teach this. I personally got caught up in it despite it not sitting right with me. Finally I searched the truth and realized the way we've been doing things isn't in the Bible at all. What I found, instead, is that victory in spiritual warfare and deliverance are, first and foremost, indicative of our *faith walk*, not some zealous determination to take a stand against the enemy, casting demons out of every situation, or binding and loosing left and right. Sure, there's a time to take authority but we've made this our futile recourse.

The phrase 'warring in the Spirit' is tossed around quite a bit and we know it refers to praying in the Spirit concerning the spiritual battle we are in. But I'm concerned that 'warring in the Spirit' is more of a subconscious advance against the enemy than anything else. We know it's an advance towards the Father in that we're praying in the Spirit (tongues). But we must be careful not to also mix it with the idea that we, ourselves, are charging, rebuking, binding or commanding the devil and his minions in the process. Holy Spirit may lead us to take authority while 'warring in the Spirit', but this is via inspiration, not a pre-determined rebuke session. There's a difference.

If we consider the finest example set for us in scripture, we see that our King spent many hours a day praying to the Father. We should take note that His time in the Secret Place was strictly about intimacy with the Father, not warring. In fact, when did Jesus ever spiritually duke things out with Satan? Never.

You already know the following but let's go over just how Jesus did deal with the devil. Satan obviously knew who the Lord was and was never so bold to approach Jesus to tempt

Him as he was during the 40 days and nights the Lord fasted in the desert. Seeing how weak and seemingly powerless Jesus was during this time led Satan to presume he might just be able to get over on the Son of Man. The prince of the air, with utmost confidence, tried three different times to defeat the Holy One. But we know that as weak as Jesus humanly was, the Word remained all powerful. All He had to do was apply the truth to the temptations and lies, and it was over. What's amazing to think about is in those moments, the One who *is* the Living Word Himself, while being countered with lies, had to *apply* the truth in order to defeat the subservient enemy.

How ironic that the Author of Life should have to apply anything to anyone! The truth is He wouldn't except that He set things up this way, and personally demonstrated that the *application of the Word* (not the mere presence of it) is what defeats evil. Think about it. Satan approached the *Living Word of God*. If the mere presence of the Word is enough to defeat darkness, the devil never would have dared to approach Jesus let alone tempt Him. Yet, he did. The presence of Jesus may have made Satan uncomfortable but it didn't halt him. Jesus had to *apply* the truth to defeat him. It's like if Satan approached your Bible and said to it, *"Throw yourself into the flames of the fireplace, the Lord your God will keep you from burning and even smelling of smoke."* Your Bible itself is a loaded gun. But Satan knows if it isn't fired by responding with the real truth, it may as well go into the flames because it's useless against him.

Let's expound upon the difference between knowing and applying the Word for a moment. Say you're driving down the road heading to an important interview. Suddenly you get a flat tire and you know you're going to be late. This isn't only frustrating because you are eager for the interview and its results; it's also tempting to be anxious as to whether or not things are going to work out now. Perhaps the employer will frown upon this and let the incident influence his decision to hire you. As frustrating as it is, you must remember that God commands us in His Word to not be anxious about anything, but in everything, by prayer and petition with thanksgiving, to present our requests to Him (Philippians 4:6). Upon recalling this truth, if anxiety is still trying to grip you, you need to speak this truth to the anxiety. Then resist it by praying with thanksgiving and presenting your request to God – and trusting Him in the matter. *Applying* the Word of God is warring against the enemy. On the contrary, not applying the truth and obeying the anxiety is obeying the devil and gives him the upper hand. Knowing the truth without applying it is shunning the power of God and gives power to darkness. If, after all, The Word Himself needed to apply the truth against the devil, how much more do we?

THE FULL ARMOR OF GOD

In addition to the King's personal reveal on how to stop Satan in his tracks, we also know that God instructs us in Ephesians 6 to put on the full armor of God. Though we get the general idea as to what this passage means, I've found that we don't *fully* get it. So let's dissect this passage:

> *"Finally, my brethren, be strong in the Lord, and in the power of his might. Put on the whole armor of God, that ye may be able to stand against the wiles of the devil. For we wrestle not against flesh and blood, but against principalities, against powers, against the rulers of the darkness of this world, against spiritual wickedness in high places. Wherefore take unto you the whole armor of God, that ye may be able to withstand in the evil day, and having done all, to stand."* Ephesians 6:10-13.

This portion of the passage is self-explanatory. It's commanding us to *be undefeated in the Lord*. Be strong in His power by wearing the protective armor of God so that when your invisible enemy charges at you, tempts you, suggests something false, tries to deceive you, you won't fall for it or buckle. You'll remain standing – steadfast and immovable.

Note that there's nothing about confronting the principalities and rulers in this passage. Take special care to realize the armor is what does the work. All you are doing in the matter is wearing it. But what, precisely, does that entail?

> *"Stand therefore, having your loins girt about with truth..."* Ephesians 6:14a.

The Hebrews wore tunic robes and had to gird them up around their loins in order to engage in battle or perform heavy labor. It was understood that girding the loins was about anticipating an attack or getting ready to fight. So the instruction to gird your loins with the truth is saying *'be prepared with resolve for the truth in anticipation of a confrontation with the liar so that when he throws the contrary at you, you won't be tripped up. You won't be lured into sin or deceived by false teaching (for example).'*

In order to not be tripped up over yourself (or tunic), you have to be resolved in the truth, not just know 'about' it. That's like having it quickly tucked, not tightly girded and securely knotted. When the lies or temptations come at you, if you aren't convinced of the truth, what you know (your tunic) will come undone and cause you to stumble. Being resolved and steadfast in the truth, however, enables you to resist the lie or temptation and win the battle.

"...and having on the breastplate of righteousness..." Ephesians 6:14b.

We know that receiving and believing in redemption through Jesus makes us righteous but also that walking upright is evidence of our faith in Christ. So this piece of armor emphasizes that this righteousness is a breastplate of protection over our hearts and souls. It's an exhortation to remain steadfast in righteousness; not doubting Jesus by yielding to sin and stepping upon His righteous covering over us. Doing so is taking off the breastplate and exposes our hearts and souls to the devil!

"And your feet shod with the preparation of the gospel of peace." Ephesians 6:15.

The gospel is the good news of the Kingdom of God, and the Bible says the Kingdom of God is righteousness, 'peace', and joy (Romans 14:17). Therefore, since the Kingdom of God is a supernatural, holy dimension, peace is likewise a supernatural, holy dimension where Satan is powerless. So the point is to always be secure in God's peace so that you are ready to respond to evil in it. The devil tries to scare or infuriate people into sin. If he can arrange the perfect storm, believers who aren't secure in God's peace will be played like violins. Yielding to strife or anxiety when Satan stirs up a storm or causes any kind of chaos is stepping out of the supernatural Kingdom of God and into the supernatural kingdom of darkness where dark powers have access to you. Stepping out of peace guarantees you will lose the battle.

If you realize this is what you have done, simply repent and step back over into the Kingdom of God – into shoes of peace where you will be safe, and God will help you recover from the brutality of the battle.

> *"Above all, taking the shield of faith, wherewith ye shall be able to quench all the fiery darts of the wicked."* Ephesians 6:16.

The Bible says faith is being *sure* of what we hope for and *certain* of what we don't see, Hebrews 11:1. This portion is saying to be so resolved about the truth that your actions reflect it. When life happens, respond in faith and confidence, not fear and insecurity. For example, if you have a child that's lost in the darkness, since you have been made righteous by the Blood of the Lamb, Proverbs 11:21 promises that your child will be delivered.

While it is painful to see the darkness in and surrounding your child, especially if they're suffering the serious consequences of their actions, rejoice that you know the *end* of the story! More than that, if they're suffering consequences, this is another sure sign that God is after them because the Bible says God chastens those that are His, Hebrews 12:6. Respond with faith, being sure of what you hope for. Your hope and guarantee is Proverbs 11:21 and Hebrews 12:6 in this matter. Therefore, everything else, including the monstrosity of their behavior, is technically irrelevant. So act like it.

This piece of armor is something many of us lay down constantly through doubt and ignorance as to what the Bible says about things. Make sure to learn what the Bible has to say about life and then be sure your actions demonstrate faith as opposed to doubt or fear. Believers who doubt and fear do not know God and His Word. To know Him and His Word is to constantly have the shield of faith up, ready and in position.

"And take the helmet of salvation..."
Ephesians 6:17.

The word 'salvation' in the New Testament (most of the time) is the Greek term sōtēria, and has to do with having been delivered or saved; such as when you are born again. There are a few times, however, where 'salvation' is actually the Greek term sōtērios and is an adjective meaning *'tending or serving to save; rescuing; preserving'*. We've assumed the helmet of salvation is the noun, sōtēria, but it's the adjective, sōtērios. This means the verse is actually saying, *"Put on the helmet that preserves, rescues and saves"*, or *"Put on the preserving helmet".*

In a nutshell, putting on the preserving helmet is cloaking the mind with truth by *convincing* our mind with the Word of God, and remaining focused on it. We can deduce that the Word of God is the preserving helmet this piece of armor is reflecting because other scriptures tell us to be transformed by the renewing of our minds (Romans 12:2) which is accomplished by consuming the Word of God. We also know the darkness attacks us through our minds (2 Corinthians 10:5) exulting itself against the knowledge (Word) of God. So blanketing our minds with the truth of God's Word is a barrier against the lies and deceptions the enemy tries to tell us. Without the preserving helmet on, we listen to the lies and believe them! With the preserving helmet on, we know better and respond with, *"Yeah, right, that's not true. I refuse to believe it."*

Knowing what the Word says isn't enough, though. Many people know scripture but forget it when things arise that contradict it, and they yield to the lies instead. Shoveling the Word into the brain through memorization, unfortunately, is not putting on the preserving helmet. Blanketing the brain with confidence and resolve for the Word is when the preserving helmet has been put on and securely fastened.

For example, Jim knows that the Bible says God is for Him and loves Him. John doesn't just know this, he believes it so much it warms him to think about it. Which one is wearing the preserving helmet? When the demons whisper to each of them, *"God's not going to show up. He doesn't care about you"*, Jim's going to bite, hook line and sinker. John's going to refute the thought and think the notion is absurd. Instead, he'll praise the Lord for how good God is instead.

"And the sword of the Spirit, which is the word of God..." Ephesians 6:17.

Of course we know this verse is saying to use the Word of God as a mighty sword against anything the enemy tries, as was demonstrated through Christ's encounter with Satan in the desert. We must know the Word so well that it's a readily available sword in our hand ready to strike against the contrary. We must be equipped to use the applicable Word on the spot. We don't always have the ability to run and look something up (search for our sword) in the face of adversity. It is best to know what applies to every situation we encounter ahead of time.

Note that the belt of truth, the shield of faith, the helmet of salvation and the sword of the Spirit all reflect knowing and *believing* the truth so emphatically that it influences how you react to and deal with life. This is no coincidence. The Lord knew we would struggle with believing and applying His truths in our everyday living. That's why *four* of the six pieces of armor exhort to not just know about the truth, but to be firm and absolutely resolved in the truth. Believing God is the primary key to our experiential victory through Him.

Also, note that the sword of the Spirit is the final piece of armor. Sure, anyone can pick up a sword and fight without wearing the rest of the armor. But this is dangerous for obvious reasons. Throwing the sword (or Word) around might nick the enemy, but why thrust when you're all exposed? That's why God says to first know the Word, firmly believing and being established in the truth, applying your faith in all things, remaining steadfast and focused on the truth ...before actually using the sword. If you're not resolved and fully confident in and fully believing the Word (meaning you're naked, without armor) yet you pick up the sword and begin refuting the devil, you're thrusts will be weak. Your jabs will miss. All the while, you'll be fully exposed to Satan's blows and darts. This is why we must be absolutely solid in our faith.

Putting it simply, the armor of God is a state of being; a condition of faith. Waking up in the morning and putting each piece on one by one may be of some benefit, but the bottom line is we need to live in this state of confident knowing. When we waiver in spiritual resolve and character, fully literate and focused on the truth, or when we don't live by the Spirit in peace and remain upright, we are vulnerable to attack and will lose many battles.

As you can see by now, our view of spiritual warfare seriously needed to be tweaked. Please realize... It's not about addressing the enemy, charging and commanding him away. It's about our faith walk and living out (*and in*) the Word. It's about unity with truth. Abiding in God puts us out of the enemy's reach where we don't have to battle. The Word is the power. Wearing the Word, being one with the Word, is wearing the full armor of God.

This is the only depiction of spiritual warfare the Bible conveys. Yes, casting out demons is an element to walking with Christ. But we must put everything into perspective. Casting out demons is not the same as spiritual warfare. Casting out demons is executing authority over a pesky spirit that's controlling or influencing someone. Spiritual warfare is being poised in the security of the Holy Kingdom, armed with truth, where no power of darkness has legitimate access to you.

-Chapter 4-

DOES CASTING OUT PYTHON *EVER* WORK?

Once you appreciate that experiential victory depends upon your faith walk, you'll appreciate more that this is how casting out demons becomes a workable thing for you.

Casting out demons is absolutely scriptural. So can we cast the spirit of python out? Buckle your seat belts. This is where things get interesting.

Remember how Jesus said He'd have to bind the strongman in order to plunder the strongman's house? Since Jesus was in the business of casting out demons, why didn't He stick with the program and say He'd have to, likewise, *cast out* the strongman in order to plunder the strongman's house? The answer is because you cannot go onto somebody else's property and tell them to leave. It would have to be a forced maneuver. Ordering Satan to leave his own territory isn't possible. That's why He'd have to bind the strong man before he could plunder him. (Note that in so doing, the instance isn't about Jesus exercising authority in binding him, rather, it's an invasion.)

With that in mind, let's talk about the kingdoms. The Bible speaks about the Kingdom of God and the kingdom of darkness. Kingdoms are governments with armies that have a hierarchy of officials and militia with various rankings. These kingdoms are invisible to us but they are very real, very powerful, and very active. They each have their own sets of opposing policies.

When people operate according to the policies of one kingdom over the other, this is the divine, governmental power they are subjecting themselves to in that moment. As much as we'd like to think we're only subject to the physical realm and its authorities, we're wrong. Every action we take is in agreement with and submission to either the Kingdom of God or the Kingdom of darkness. Fortunately, Jesus provided a "Get out of Satan's kingdom free" card. And it works via genuine repentance. Unfortunately, we willfully choose to stay there – knowingly or not. Or we don't repent.

Despite being invisible, both of these kingdoms are territorial. Obeying their policies, then, is stepping into their territory. Again, this means in any given moment, whatever you're doing is either compliance with the dark kingdom or compliance with the Kingdom of God and is subjecting yourself to their rulers and divine authorities. It's the same as how things work in the physical realm. You may be a citizen of Ohio but if you visit Kentucky, you are subject to the laws in Kentucky while you're there. If what you're doing while in Kentucky is against that state's law regardless if it's legal in Ohio, you will suffer the consequences.

Now let's talk about the spirit of python and how he fits into all this. As I disclosed previously, the spirit of python is the false prophet, the counterfeit of the Holy Spirit. Python and the antichrist are in the highest positions under Satan. And their jobs are to lure believers into operating according to dark kingdom policies. They do this so that they acquire legal access. In python's case, his goal is to constrict you, as we talked about earlier. Regardless what strategies he implements and which demons he uses to accomplish it.

Now the thing is... Python knows he has to get you to willfully come over into dark kingdom territory. Sure, he knows you're saved. But if he can get you to agree with him or yield to something false, he knows he acquires *legal* access to you. Even if just temporarily. You may be a citizen of heaven but you're touchable while hanging out in dark domain.

When you agree with the false prophet in any way, shape or form... When you bow to any idol or love something more than God... When you believe and practice any type of false doctrine or teaching... When you willfully do or believe anything that is a dark kingdom policy, you are visiting and subject to dark kingdom authorities. You have stepped out of the safety of God's Kingdom over into the danger zone.

Since this is the case, how can you cast the spirit of python out? How can you cast any demon out that you willfully agreed with or bowed down to?

Imagine if a vindictive, abusive neighbor comes over to your house, enters and begins verbally assaulting you. You have every right and the authority to tell him to leave. If he refuses, you can call for higher authorities to assist you to get him out. On the contrary, if the same abusive neighbor invites you in, if you're foolish enough to enter his domain and he starts verbally assaulting you, you can't tell him to leave. You have to leave. Try to call the police to have him put out all you want – it won't work. It's precisely the same with the invisible authorities. If you willfully step onto their domain, how can you cast them out? Call on Jesus to get the demons away from you all you want – it won't work. You're the one that has to leave via repentance.

The problem with some deliverance ministries is ministers with legitimate authority (though, we find that very few walk in it) is if they cut off python's head or cast him out, he's not going to budge because you're the one in dark kingdom territory. Not the other way around. You are the one that has to do the exiting. Ministers do often discern that you are the one that opened the door via a particular area of sin or unbelief so they'll work with you to repent and close the door to that spirit. This is right on, but the next question is what if deep down you still carry approval for it? Yes, you sincerely repented and hate your sin. But what if you don't yet own the truth of what God says concerning the matter? This means this area that was cleaned out remains empty and the spirits can and will come back – with seven more!

Commanding a demon, python or even Satan to leave is only possible when THEY are the ones trespassing into Kingdom of God territory to try to ensnare or assault you. But as you can see now, this isn't usually the case. The powers of darkness have been at work against the Church for millennia; they're smart. They know they're better off getting you over into their territory where they can legally have a hay day with you. They only resort to trespassing onto God's domain when you aren't biting and going over to them. But this is rarely necessary because we've been bowing to their every suggestion, handing them our fate on silver platters. Then wondering why God isn't showing up – clueless that we're the ones who stepped away from God. *We are the ones choosing God but failing to become one with Him and His truths, leaving ourselves vulnerable to the enemy's strategies.*

When believers buckle down and zero in on Jesus, learn His policies inside and out and live them, the spirit of python *has no ground*. That's when he gets desperate and will look for ways to send troops over into Holy Kingdom territory in hopes that you won't notice and kick them out. But they're very nervous about doing so because believers who don't dabble with the dark kingdom are typically well versed in the Word of God and will discern the evil spirits, and cast them out. Dark powers will only attempt what they think they're likely to get away with.

So, believers who are oppressed and constricted by the spirit of python are most likely subject to the authority of the dark kingdom on account of the policies they're abiding by. Sometimes there are generational spirits that haven't been broken that have nothing to do with the believer personally. But not all that often because since the believer (who has the power of the blood of Jesus already covering them) rejects the false policy himself his forefather's yielded to, this severs the legal access. Those particular generational spirits, then, are illegally trespassing and need to be told to go. –They bank on never being told to, however. That's why they stick around even when their legal rights have been nullified in the high courts of Heaven.

To reiterate, the only way the spirit of python can legally have dominion over a believer is if the believer is operating according to dark kingdom policies – wittingly or unwittingly. If the believer isn't, however, that's when python must be kicked off the property. Colossians 1:13 says believers have absolutely been rescued from the dominion of darkness and transferred into the Kingdom of God's dear Son. It's a done deal. But believing Jesus means obeying God's policies. Disobeying them is revisiting the kingdom you were rescued from which grants the enemy rights again. And the only way to cut them off, again, is to repent and turn from the sin, again.

    The problem is most believers don't understand how they're yielding to dark kingdom policies. It could be something as simple as having self-pity on account of harsh, relentless injustice. Though the pain is legitimate, we don't need to feel sorry for ourselves when we have Jesus. Yes, that sounds cliché. But it's the truth. *"Though they slay me, yet will I trust Him,"* Job 13:15. Feeling great about Jesus and eternity with Him should so fill us that the horrific pains of this life don't cause us to feel sorry for ourselves. The Lord warned us we would have troubles in this world. Why do we get so distraught over them? Feeling sorry for ourselves is a policy of darkness – regardless how legitimate the pain is that we face. It's never justified despite how justified *we feel*. It's the same with feeling bitter about a crappy situation, being jealous, worrying about the bills, etc. These may seem to be justifiable responses to bad things going on, but these aren't Holy Kingdom policies. God's policies include trusting Him, focusing on the eternal, rejoicing, thanking Him despite the uncertainties of this life, and enduring through the garbage. We think because we obey the big stuff by not cussing, smoking, drugging, drinking, fornicating, murdering, etc., that we're in the clear. But that's not the case. Anything we do that is contrary to what the Bible says, including worry about a bill, is operating according to dark kingdom policies.

The exciting news is Holy Spirit does an EXCELLENT job showing us which dark kingdom policies we abide by – if we're open to face the truth, that is. But that's the key. We have to be sincerely willing to find out plus diligently work with Him and read the Word to gain further understanding as to where we're going wrong. I've discovered too many people, including myself, are afraid to be wrong. We have to get over that!

Few of us, if any, rise to perfection. We all stumble to one degree or another. And yes, if we don't repent, we've granted the enemy access. So, the key to victory over the spirit of python and every foul entity roaming about the planet, is first and foremost, to secure our faith walk, knowing and owning the truth, living it, and applying it, all the while working with Holy Spirit on coming out of agreement with darkness, repenting and closing the doors. On one hand this sounds very simple. On another hand it may sound daunting. I admit, it is a process and requires diligence. It requires shutting the world out and becoming one with God. The more one we become with God, the more experiential victory over darkness we walk in! But it's possible. I did it and you can do it, too.

Forget casting out demons and cutting off python's head for now. If you want to cut him off... *resist him!* Work on getting out and *staying* out of dark kingdom territory. When you have evidence that the Kingdom of God is thriving in you (which is righteousness, peace and joy) and when you have born much fruit of the Spirit (again, peace in the storms, joy despite pain, patience with those who are unnerving, love for those you can't stand, kindness with idiots, humility with the arrogant, self-control in chaos, etc.) and you know you are operating according to God's policies, Holy Spirit will *then* instruct you to tell a particular spirit to get off your property. Otherwise, steer clear of casting out demons. Be sure it's the leading of the Holy Spirit and you aren't the one dabbling in their policies.

Whether you agree with Lonnie Lane's teaching that binding and loosing in Hebrew is actually forbidding and permitting, or whether you agree that there's no clear indication in the Bible that binding and loosing is a right thing to do... I advise against it until you know for sure you aren't the one hanging out in the dark kingdom. Remember, scripture exhorts us to KNOW and BE RESOLVED IN the Word of God, applying it, living it, standing on it, and focusing on it always. This is becoming one with God and is what defeats every power of hell.

Final Words

In summary, remember that the ever so popular doctrine of binding and loosing isn't in the Bible. God Himself never applied such restraints to demons. The angels God bound weren't spirits, and the Bible only speaks of binding Satan in chains for 1,000 years to the Abyss. That's it. The other binding and loosing passages actually speak to forbidding or approving spiritual matters of the Church. When it comes to *forbidding a spirit*, Holy Spirit can certainly use the term "binding" to do so, perhaps. But this would be in conjunction with showing it the door. Binding is not some standard protocol like it was made out to be when it comes to dealing with darkness. No, we've got that all wrong. It was never a concept outlined in the Bible or implemented by the Kingdom of God in the way we see that believers are doing these days. Casting evil powers out is the primary course of action (when we're not the ones in their territory). Forbidding (binding them), if ever, would only be applicable under the primary protocol of making demons leave.

Finally, casting out demons is the defensive recourse taken when the offensive recourse of being aligned with truth is put into order first. Understand that casting out demons absolutely works – *for those who are not frequenting dark kingdom territory, who are operating and living in alignment with God and His policies, for those who live in the full armor of God (His Word), for those who are about God's business, and for those who aren't tangled up with the thorns of this life.*

Indeed, though people who walk like this with God seem perfect, they aren't. Remember, it's about where the person abides, where there confidence lies, whose ways and kingdom principles they yield to in given situations. Such believers aren't perfect, but they generally hang out in Truthville and resist suggestions and temptations of darkness on the norm. If and when they do falter, they respond to the conviction of the Holy Spirit, repent, and get back on the horse. Repentance keeps them from losing authority. The devil knows such resolved, repentant believers are still plugged into the power source of His Majesty by virtue of the Blood of Christ and their submission to Him, despite their blunders.

The other aspect to having no authority or victory against python and all the spirits he employs has to do with how we believe. Many Christians do believe Jesus is the Risen Lord Who reigns Supreme over the Kingdom of God. But they have faulty confidence (which is lack of faith and belief) in certain areas. Believing

God (which is demonstrated in our actions and reactions to life) concerning all that He is and says is where the power to defeat darkness is manifest.

For many who are not only unable to cast out demons but are adversely pummeled by darkness, their recourse is to get out of dark kingdom territory FIRST. A simple self-examination of one's reactions to this life and whether they demonstrate trust in God, confidence, security, peace, and endurance, is a good way to identify which kingdom one is adhering to most. Working one on one with Holy Spirit and recognizing all errors, unbelief, false perspectives and all else will also help bring one out from abiding in the dark kingdom. Repenting and turning from operating in the policies of hell is the key to overcoming. And walking with resolve in God's policies, instead, relinquishes all the powers of hell that have been successful at oppressing their lives.

The bottom line is the spirit of python, all his cohorts, and even the devil himself, have no authority over people who are one with God. Their actions, which reflect confidence and resolve in Christ and all He says, is a barrier against python. He can try to touch such a child of God, but their unity with Christ's truth deflects his efforts. They won't receive or believe his lies and they aren't so easily tempted – which are python's only avenues.

Unless God overrides this and gives Satan special permission to pummel such believers like He did to Job, the enemy can't succeed against them.

The biggest thing to walk away from this title with is that the spirit of python isn't an enemy to be bound. Rather, he's a high power that the believer needs to stop bowing to in order to overcome him. These spirits and their high princes are free to roam the earth and pursue their victims, otherwise, God would have bound them by now and wouldn't wait until after the Great Tribulations. Our job as children of God is to simply know God intimately so that we aren't accessible targets; and also so that we can effectively contend with them via Christ's authority by casting them out, when necessary.

Printed in Great Britain
by Amazon